DATE DUE

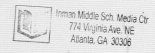

RESPECT OTHERS, RESPECT YOURSELF!

Sarah Medina

Heinemann Library
Chicago, Illinois

www.heinemannraintree.com
Visit our website to find out more information about Heinemann-Raintree books.

To order:
☎ Phone 888-454-2279
🖳 Visit www.heinemannraintree.com
to browse our catalog and order online.

© 2009 Heinemann Library
an imprint of Capstone Global Library, LLC
Chicago, Illinois

Customer Service: 888-454-2279

Visit our website at
www.heinemannraintree.com

Edited by Harriet Milles and Adam Miller
Designed by Philippa Jenkins and Artistix
Picture research by Elizabeth Alexander
Production by Victoria Fitzgerald

Printed and bound in China by South China
  Printing Company Ltd.

13 12 11 10 09
10 9 8 7 6 5 4 3 2 1

Library of Congress Cataloging-in-Publication Data
Medina, Sarah, 1960-
  Respect others, respect yourself / Sarah Medina.
-- 1st ed.
      p. cm. -- (Life skills)
  Includes bibliographical references and index.
  ISBN 978-1-4329-2723-3 (hc)
  1. Respect. I. Title.
  BJ1533.R4.M43 2009
  179'.9--dc22
                              2008047824

Acknowledgments
The author and publishers are grateful to the following for permission to reproduce copyright material: © Alamy pp. **47** (Angela Hampton/ Bubbles Photolibrary), **5** (Art Kowalsky), **31** (Jim West), **35** (Mike Greenslade), **38–39** (Richard Levine), **33** (Sally and Richard Greenhill), **20** (Vario images GmbH & Co.KG/Ulrich Baumgarten); © Corbis pp. **37** (Ecoscene/ Anthony Cooper), **29** (Imagesource), **19** (Thinkstock), **16** (Tim Pannell), **22** (Will & Deni McIntyre); © Getty Images pp. **7** (Stone/David Young-Wolff), **25** (Stone/Sean Justice), **43** (The Image Bank/Blasius Erlinger); © iStockphoto p. **26**; © Masterfile/Jon Feingersh p. **9**; © Photolibrary pp. **11** (Flint Collection/Randy Faris), **12** (Index Stock Imagery/Jentz David), **49** (Jack Hollingsworth/Photodisc), **44–45** (Japack), **15** (Ryan McVay/Photodisc);© Rex Features/ John Powell p. **40**.

Cover photograph of a teenage girl looking annoyed reproduced with permission of © Shutterstock/Margot Petrowski.

We would like to thank Robin Lomas for his invaluable help in the preparation of this book.

Every effort has been made to contact copyright holders of material reproduced in this book. Any omissions will be rectified in subsequent printings if notice is given to the publishers.

Contents

Some words are printed in bold, **like this**. You can find out what they mean by looking in the glossary.

Respect: The Best Starting Point

Mutual respect helps to make families, friendships, schools, and the community work more smoothly. It makes the world a better place.

RESPECTING OTHERS

Jack likes reading and classical music, and there is nothing he hates more than running around chasing a ball on a soccer field. The other boys at school give Jack a hard time: "What a geek!" or "He's a wimp!" They have no respect for Jack.

We all have many relationships in our lives, with family and friends, with classmates and teachers at school, and with people in the community. If any of these people treat us badly—if they are rude or hurtful, don't listen to us, or don't take us seriously—we feel bad. If we do that to them, they feel bad, too!

Equal value

If people treat us well and make us feel valued and important, it is a whole different story. We feel good, not only about ourselves, but also about life in general. And the same goes for them. When you respect other people you behave decently and politely toward them, no matter what they look like, what they have or don't have, or what they do or don't do. You are tolerant and accepting of others.

You recognize that everyone is of equal value in this world, and everyone deserves to be treated with dignity.

The starting point for respecting others is understanding that everyone is different—and that no one is better than anyone else.

Respecting yourself

Respect leads to good relationships. Lack of respect leads to damaged relationships, **abuse**, bullying, and **antisocial behavior**.

Fortunately, Jack has a healthy dose of self-respect. Even though he gets bullied for being different, he knows that it is the **bullies** who have the problem—not him. He is content with who he is. He has no intention of changing his interests just for the sake of "fitting in."

If you respect yourself, you feel happy in your own skin. You know that you are unique and have a special place in the world. When you understand your own value, it is easier for you to see the value in other people. And this is when respect for others can truly begin.

A wider perspective

Respect is about people—but it is not just about people. Respect comes from valuing everything that is important. This includes property, the environment, and the world we live in.

This book looks at all these different aspects of respect: self-respect, respect for others, and respect for the wider world. It shows the difference that respect can make to our lives, and to the lives of others.

Mutual respect makes it easier for people to inhabit the world happily together.

Self-Respect

Self-respect is important, and it helps you to truly respect others. When you respect yourself, you know your own value. This helps you to see the value in other people. You expect respect from others—and you respect them in return.

What is Self-Respect?

When you have self-respect, you basically like yourself. You may not like all aspects of your personality or everything you do. Maybe you find it hard to focus on your homework, which gets you into trouble at school. But you know that no one is perfect, and that you can change things if you need to. The great thing is that you do not beat yourself up about having weaknesses. It is only human!

Self-respect is not about liking yourself for what you can do (for instance, being good at sports or tests) or what you own (the latest MP3 player or trendy new jeans). It is about liking yourself for who you are.

What others say

When you have self-respect, you do not rely on other people to make you feel good about yourself. You love a compliment, just like everyone else. But you know your own worth, without needing to hear it from others.

Getting it Right

Connor used to love junk food. After school, he used to sit down in front of the television and fill up on chips, chocolate, and soda drinks. The trouble is, Connor also loved sports. He dreamed of being a professional basketball player—but he was not fit enough to make it through to half-time! One day, he decided enough was enough. He needed to make some changes. He cut out the junk, started to exercise, and practiced his basketball skills with his friends at every opportunity. The day came when Connor was chosen to play on his school team. He was on his way to reaching his goal.

If someone tells you that you are lazy, it can make you feel pretty miserable. Criticism can be hard to swallow! But if you respect yourself, you do not feel threatened by criticism. You think about what has been said, and you make up your own mind about it. If you accept the criticism, you make changes. If not, you forget about it. You have the confidence to make your own decisions and not to be swayed by what others say.

When you are happy with who you are, you respect yourself.

Lacking self-respect

People who lack self-respect sometimes focus too much on trying to please other people. But respect is about recognizing your own worth, as well as the worth of others. When you have self-respect, you help other people with their needs, but you never ignore your own.

Self-care

Having self-respect helps you to be confident, successful, and happy throughout your life. When you respect yourself, you know how to take care of yourself and make decisions that are good for you.

Self-respect is about valuing yourself. And, when you value yourself, you take care of yourself to the best of your ability. You care for your body by resting enough, eating well, exercising, and avoiding unhealthy substances. You care for your mind by learning as much as you can in school and developing your talents. You care for your emotions by making sure that people know what you think and feel.

Positive talk

When you respect yourself, you say and think positive things about yourself. Instead of saying, "I'm terrible at tennis," you say something like, "I'm a lot better at volleyball than tennis. But I really like tennis, and I'm working hard on my technique, so hopefully I'll improve soon."

Because you feel comfortable with yourself, you are not afraid to get things wrong. You know this is one of the best ways to learn. And because you are confident about your own strengths, you are happy to say what you think, and you do not compare yourself negatively with others.

The feel-good factor

When you have self-respect, you make sure that you spend time doing things you enjoy and are good at—or that you want to become good at. You may set yourself goals—for instance, to play a particular sport every day, or read a new book every week. You have fun, keep your confidence high, and feel good. You hang out with people who like you and who treat you well. And you never let people put you down.

I'm OK; you're OK

When you respect yourself, you know that you are important—but you also know that the world does not revolve around you! Other people are important, too. You do not judge others; you try to understand them, no matter how different they are from you. You respect them for who they are and treat them politely. You also think about how the things you do might affect someone else. This helps to build strong, healthy relationships.

Developing self-respect

Self-respect is something we learn, not something we are born with. We first learn about self-respect from our parents or caregivers. If we do not learn self-respect at home, we can still develop it as we get older. We all meet many people throughout our lives who can be excellent role models for self-respect. We can watch, talk to, and learn a lot from them.

Self-respect and respect for others leads to good relationships and lasting friendships.

Respect in Families

Families are very important for shaping how we feel about ourselves and other people. If we are fortunate, our parents and caregivers love and respect us, and help us to develop self-respect. Sadly, respect in some families is missing. People in these families need to learn self-respect and respect for others in a different way—at school, or with friends or other relatives, for example. Fortunately, life gives us many opportunities for learning about respect.

DID YOU KNOW?

All families are different! Some families are "traditional," with two parents who live together with their children. Some are single-parent families, with just one parent caring for the children. Others are step-families, where parents have **divorced** and formed new relationships. Some children grow up in adoptive families or extended families. Each family has its own way of doing things—ideally, with respect right at its heart. When respect is central in a family, all family members feels good about themselves and know their unique value. Loving parents and caregivers build their children's self-respect—helping them to learn about respect for others, too.

TEACHING SELF-RESPECT

Good parents and caregivers teach self-respect in many ways. They love their children and are kind, thoughtful, and respectful toward them. They accept that their children are individuals, and they give them lots of praise and attention. They encourage their children to do well, but they are not pushy. They teach their children right from wrong and trust their children to do the right thing.

Good parents and caregivers are always fair. They may get annoyed with some of the things their children do and they may **discipline** them. But they listen to their children's thoughts and feelings, too. They keep their promises, and they are honest and not afraid to say "Sorry" when they have made a mistake. They are also polite, saying "Please" and "Thank you" to everyone at home, both young and old.

Teaching respect for others

When parents and caregivers teach self-respect, they also teach children to respect others. This is because they are teaching by example; everything they do comes from respecting their children. And children learn more from watching what others do than by what they are told.

In a perfect world, all parents and caregivers know the importance of showing and teaching respect at home. In the real world, this does not always happen. Some people have never learned to respect themselves—and this makes it hard for them to respect others or to teach their children self-respect.

Whether your family is large or small, respect helps family relationships to run more smoothly.

Respecting relatives

There can be lots of relatives in a family: parents or caregivers, brothers and sisters, aunts, uncles, cousins, and grandparents. You sometimes need to show respect to different relatives in different ways. You might be very casual with your **siblings**, but need to talk politely to your grandparents.

Each person is different, and you may get along better with some relatives than others. But all family members deserve to be respected! You may find some harder to get along with than others. Some may annoy you. But remember that their opinions and feelings (and in the case of your parents or caregivers, their workloads) deserve as much respect as your own.

Respect for your family can often be shown in practical ways, such as doing simple chores like washing the family car—without being asked to do it!

Rules—why bother?

Some parents and caregivers have house rules—about bedtimes, mealtimes, and housework, for example—that they expect their children to follow. If you are watching a DVD, it can be annoying to be asked to do the dishes. But respecting rules and expectations at home helps us to deal with rules at school and in society, too. And learning to get along with your family is great practice for getting along with other people throughout your life.

In a world where millions of people live together in society, rules help life to run more smoothly. They are there to help people to know what to do and to stay safe. It would be chaos if no one respected traffic lights, for example. Vehicles would crash, people would be injured or killed, and no one would ever get to where they need to go!

Getting it Right

People think that communication is about saying what you think—but it is as much about listening as talking! To communicate well, you need to stay calm and speak quietly and respectfully. You need to listen to what other people have to say and try to see things from their point of view. That way, you can negotiate the best way forward.

TIP

Sometimes you may disagree with one or more house rule. Perhaps you want to stay up later on weekends. Talking to your parent or caregiver will help to resolve any differences in opinion. It is a big part of building good relationships, too.

If you can understand why rules are needed, it can help you to respect your house rules more easily. Rules about housework, for example, mean that everyone who lives in the home and benefits from home life shares in the work that is needed to keep it running. This gives everyone some time to relax and have fun, too. If you think about it, it is crazy and inefficient for just one family member to have to spend several hours per week doing all the household chores when the work could be achieved in less than half the time by everyone in the family helping out.

13

Respecting siblings

You may love your brothers or sisters, but it does not mean that you always get along well. Respecting someone who is so close to you, but possibly quite different, can take some effort. But it is well worth it. Sibling relationships can be the best, most fun, and most loving relationships you have in your life!

If your sister wears your top without asking, you might feel pretty annoyed. If you tease your brother in front of his friends, he might feel humiliated. Sometimes siblings do not treat each other fairly. Because they live together, they take each other for granted. Unfortunately, they often end up treating one another in ways that they would never treat other people.

DID YOU KNOW?

Sibling rivalry is when brothers and sisters argue and even fight with each other. They may be jealous of each other, thinking that the other gets more attention and love from parents and caregivers. Sometimes the problems come from each person wanting to have his or her own space, or from belongings being taken without asking.

Sibling rivalry can be very upsetting—but it can be resolved. As with all relationships, good communication (see page 13) can help siblings to work out their differences and get along better with each other.

Learning how to respect and get along with a sibling is a great way to learn the skills we need to get along with the many other people we meet throughout life. We do not need to receive respect to give respect. But when we keep giving respect, we will eventually find that we are respected in return.

Respect for siblings is about thinking of what they need and want. Speak to them politely, ask before you borrow their things, and knock before going into their room. Remember that small actions can lead to big rewards.

When siblings enjoy each other's company, they build up good memories—and mutual respect.

Erin and her brother Mike were given a box of chocolates to share. When Erin craved a chocolate, she went to the box— only to find that greedy Mike had eaten them all! Erin was upset and angry. She thought that Mike had behaved selfishly and disrespectfully.

Erin could have screamed and yelled at her brother and dragged their parents into the argument. She was tempted to do this, but decided that it would only make things worse. Instead, she calmly told Mike how upset and annoyed she felt. She asked him why he didn't save any chocolates for her. In the end, they agreed that the next time a box of goodies came their way, they would split them right away. That way, they would each have their fair share.

Respecting grandparents

You are very fortunate if you have grandparents. They have had a lot of life experience, and they can teach you a lot about how to get along with people and how to make good decisions. You just need to be willing to listen!

The age difference between you and your grandparents can bring special challenges. Life was very different when your grandparents were young, and they may expect you to behave in ways that you do not like or understand. If they ask you to turn your music down, for example, try to understand their point of view.

Understanding each other is the key to respectful relationships between grandparents and grandchildren. Age has nothing to do with it— old and young people can and should respect each other equally.

A respectful relationship between you and your grandparents can enrich your life.

IS RESPECT WORKING IN YOUR FAMILY?

1) **Your dad says that you can't go out with your friend on the weekend. You:**
   a) go crazy! Tell him his rules are stupid—and then storm off to your room.
   b) say OK. Then tell a lie and sneak out to see your friend anyway.
   c) talk to your dad calmly and **compromise**. Find out why he doesn't want you to go—then explain why it is important to you.

2) **Your sister wants to use your makeup, but you don't want her to. You:**
   a) tell her to get lost. It's not her stuff and she can't have it!
   b) let her use it, but then wear some of her clothes without asking.
   c) say OK, she can borrow it. But ask her to be careful with it and give it back to you right away.

3) **Your grandma scolds you for putting your elbows on the table during dinner at her house. You:**
   a) ignore her. Your mom doesn't expect you to do that, so why should she?
   b) do what she says, but spend the rest of dinner sulking.
   c) do as she asks, because you know it will make her happy. Ask her why so that you can understand her point of view.

4) **Your little brother keeps bothering you when you are trying to do your homework. You:**
   a) yell at him to go away and leave you alone.
   b) stop doing your homework. Who cares if it's late?
   c) ask him to give you some space for a while and tell him you will definitely play with him later.

See quiz results on page 50.

Respect in Friendships

We meet and make lots of friends throughout our lives. Some friendships come and go, and others last a lifetime—but all our friendships are important.

LOOKING OUT FOR OUR FRIENDS

Friends bring something fresh and interesting to our lives. We grow up with our families, and we know them really well. Our friends may be very different, and they can teach us new ideas. We may have new, interesting experiences with them. Good friends help and support us, too. With our friends, we can explore who we are and who we want to be.

Mutual respect between friends is essential. Without respect, friendships can be difficult—and can break down completely. Good friends see themselves as equals and treat each other with the respect this brings. If friends do not think about each other's wants and needs, they may lose the friendship. If they do not communicate well, it can be hard to resolve problems.

Another important aspect of a good friendship is the ability to accept one another's differences. No two friends (or group of friends) are ever going to think exactly alike in all possible situations. However, it is true that some differences will go too deep for you to be able to resolve and may break your friendship.

Getting respect right with friends

You can show your friends that you respect them by listening to their ideas. Maybe you want to go ice skating, but your friend would rather go to a movie. Be prepared to compromise; do what others like to do sometimes, and what you want to do at other times. It is called "give and take," and it helps to build good relationships.

Trying to control whom other people see and what they do is not respectful. If a friend wants to go out with another friend, let her! Put yourself in her shoes—would you like to be made to feel bad because you want to be alone or see someone else? Remember that respect is about accepting our differences, even when we would rather our friends were just the same as us.

Sometimes taking the time to just listen is the best way to respect a friend.

If friends have problems, do your best to help them. You could do something hands-on, like helping them with homework. Or you can simply be there for them, giving them your time, listening to them, and finding out what they need most. You should always respect your friends if they do not want to talk about their problems. Doing something fun with them can take their mind off things for a while. If they do want to talk, make sure to listen to them carefully. It is not respectful to bombard them with your own views and feelings. Listening is more important than talking! If they show their feelings—by crying, for example—don't worry; let them be. Ask them if they need help from a trusted adult. If they say yes, you can help them to talk to the right person to get the support they need.

Negative peer pressure

People often change as they get older. One of your friends might start hanging out with new people. He or she may do things you don't like—such as missing classes, smoking, or experimenting with drugs or alcohol.

Sometimes a friend may try to persuade you to do something you don't want to do. This is negative **peer pressure**. It may make you feel worried or annoyed. If you go along with it, it could lead to trouble. Negative peer pressure is not respectful because it ignores your feelings and your individuality.

If you experience negative pressure from friends, it is worth talking to them about how it makes you feel. They may stop pressuring you, and you may be able to persuade them to do the right thing, too. If this does not work, you may need to move away. Remember, good friends respect who you are—just as you are.

Getting it
Wrong

Adam used to go to the skateboard park with his friends after school. They worked on their skills and had a good time. Then one day he found his friends spraying graffiti on the slopes. Adam didn't like this; it made him feel uncomfortable. He just wanted to skateboard, and this was no fun. But his friends made fun of him and called him boring. They said he was chicken and he should run home to his mom. Adam felt embarrassed. He picked up a can and sprayed his name next to theirs. And then they were caught . . .

It can be too easy to act without thinking. If you are on the verge of losing your temper, take a deep breath and think about how you can use respect to resolve the problem instead.

Defusing arguments

It is perfectly normal for friends to argue sometimes. If you know you have done or said something wrong, it is respectful to be honest and to say "Sorry." However, shouting is not respectful—and neither is storming off in a rage. Good communication is essential for good friendships (see page 13) and will generally help to resolve friendship problems.

Always try to listen to what your friends have to say—no matter how angry you feel, or however "wrong" you think they are. Then ask yourself: "Am I being fair? Do they actually have a point?"

When you respect people, you value them for who they are. You do not care about what they look like or what they wear. What they have or don't have is not important. Telling your friends that you like them, or showing them by doing something nice for them, is a great way to show respect and strengthen your friendships. Remember that good friends are very special, and you need to treat them with care.

"Never impose on others what you would not choose for yourself."

From The Analects of Confucius
[Confucius was a Chinese philospher, who lived 551–479 BCE.]

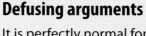

Self-respect in friendships

Respecting our friends makes friendships stronger. But respect is a two-way street. We should give and receive respect in equal measure. Our needs are as important as our friends' needs. Keeping your self-respect in friendships is very important.

If friends are disrespectful to you, you should not be afraid to tell them how you feel. It is hurtful to feel that friends are not listening to you, or to find out that they have been talking about you behind your back, for example. Everyone has the right to ask for what they need. Learning about **assertiveness** can help you to do this.

Knowing that your views and opinions are listened to, valued, and respected is an important aspect of good friendships.

 **DO YOU RESPECT YOUR FRIENDS? AND DO THEY RESPECT YOU?**

1) Your friend told you she was sick, but you found out later that she was at another friend's house. You:
a) tell her you don't mind; you don't own her! But say you don't like it that she lied to you.
b) shout and say you don't ever want to see her again.
c) stay in your room and cry, and refuse to pick up the phone when she calls.

2) Your friends want you to drink alcohol with them. You don't want to. You:
a) tell them that underage drinking isn't for you. Say calmly that you don't want to get involved, even if they do.
b) get angry and walk away, telling them they're stupid.
c) feel embarrassed, but join in.

3) A friend cries and tells you she's had a big argument with her best friend. You:
a) hear her out, and encourage her to make up. Offer to talk to her friend with her, if she wants.
b) tell her to stop crying and list all the reasons why you think her friend is a waste of space.
c) listen to her, but secretly feel happy because now she can be your best friend instead!

4) Your friend really wants to watch a televison show at home, but you want to go to the school dance. You:
a) decide together to watch the show, then go to the dance later.
b) tell your friend you are going whether he is or not.
c) stay in and watch the television show, but make your friend feel bad that you are missing out.

See quiz results on page 50.

23

Respect at School

We all go through school and, if we are lucky, it can be one of the best times in our life. School teaches us a lot—not only to prepare for our future, but also about relationships with the different people we meet in and outside school. Respecting teachers and other students at school helps us to get the most out of our relationships in the wider world.

Respect for Teachers

School also presents us with a set of rules we have to learn to respect. Perhaps we have to wear a school uniform, even though we hate it! There are also rules about what we can and cannot do in the classroom and on school grounds.

As we go through school, we have to work with lots of different teachers in different subject areas. We may like and get along better with some of them than others, depending on whether their personality is similar to ours. We cannot like everyone—but respecting people does not depend on how well we get along with them. Respect stands alone, and teachers deserve as much respect as we give other people in our lives.

Teachers often have different styles of working. Some teachers are very strict. They may insist on complete silence during class. They may do most of the talking in class. Other teachers are more relaxed. These teachers may allow students to talk as they work—as long as noise levels do not get out of hand. They may allow students to lead discussions on their own some of the time.

Whatever a teacher's style is like, all teachers have certain expectations of their students. They expect them to listen to instructions and to play a full part in class. This is because they care about their students and want them to have the best possible chance of doing as well as they can.

Teaching can be a difficult job, and teachers often work long hours. They have to prepare their lesson plans and grade homework and tests. They may have large classes to teach. If they have disruptive students in class, this can make their job even harder.

When students are well-prepared for classes, pay attention, and participate fully, it makes everyone's life easier. With mutual respect, teachers and students can get the most out of their time at school.

↑ *Messing around in class is disrespectful to your teachers and classmates—and to yourself.*

Getting it **Right**

Teaching is a very rewarding profession, but it is also one of the hardest jobs on the planet! Making sure that all students are given the information and skills they need to pass important tests and move confidently into the adult world is a huge responsibility. Like the rest of us, teachers have bad days once in a while. Their jobs involve a lot of work and pressure, and sometimes they get stressed. Try to respect your teachers. Understand that they want the best for you—and, just like you, they are only human!

RESPECT FOR CLASSMATES

It is as important to respect our classmates as it is to respect our teachers. If we do not respect our classmates, it can lead to conflict and unhappiness, as people get annoyed and argue with one another. If just two people in a class have problems with each other and make this obvious in class, it can disrupt the whole group. This makes learning much harder.

You can respect your classmates by being quiet in class, so that others can concentrate; by taking part fully in class work, so everyone can get the most out of it; and by listening carefully to others' views, so they feel that their contribution is important. Making fun of classmates has no part in respect. Respect is about being open to everyone and being prepared to learn from them.

Respecting your classmates does not depend on you being the same.

Respect for other school students

We meet many different people in school. Some students are older than us; others are younger. Some students are **immigrants**. Different students may practice different **faiths**. They may look and act differently from us. Some students may have **disabilities**, such as learning difficulties or a physical disability that means they use a wheelchair.

No matter what other students are like, they deserve our respect. Excluding people because they are different is disrespectful and hurtful. It is also short-sighted, because we have so much to learn from people who are not the same as us.

Getting it Right

Emilia came to the United States when she was 12. She was born in Venezuela, and Spanish was her first language. She was very nervous when she started her new school because she didn't know anyone, and she was worried that she would not fit in. Although Emilia spoke a little English, she knew she had a lot to learn.

Emilia's teacher asked Jenny to spend time with Emilia during her first week at school, to help her to settle in. Jenny didn't speak Spanish, but she worked hard to understand Emilia as much as she could. She didn't laugh at Emilia's mistakes, but made her feel special and welcome and introduced Emilia to her own friends. In no time at all, Emilia felt part of the group. Her confidence grew, her English improved, and she soon felt happy in her new school. The respect Jenny gave her made a whole world of difference to Emilia's experience of the United States and her new school.

Emilia was fortunate to have someone like Jenny to be her friend. And it was a two-way street—Jenny gained a fun, interesting new friend. She learned lots about life in Venezuela and she even learned a little Spanish. Now Emilia's family has invited Jenny to join them for a trip to Venezuela to visit Emilia's grandparents. Jenny is saving every penny!

SCHOOL BULLieS

Maybe you have seen someone's schoolbag being thrown on the floor, or someone brought to tears by teasing or name-calling. Maybe you have seen bullies kicking or punching their victim. Bullying is frightening to suffer and horrible to watch. Sadly, it is all too common. In the United States, one survey showed that 28 percent of kids are bullied at school.

Bullies often pick on people who are different from them—who either look different or who have different strengths or weaknesses. They attack them physically, or with spoken or written words. Bullies have zero respect for their victim. They do not see them as an individual or consider their needs and feelings. They see them as a target, plain and simple.

Bullying causes terrible pain to victims. It can hurt people both physically and emotionally, and the consequences can last for many years. Bullying can be very dangerous. Some victims of bullying become so unhappy that they take their own lives.

Self-respect at school

We have seen the importance of self-respect throughout life. When you respect yourself at school, you do things and choose friends that make you feel good. If you have a problem with a teacher or another student, you use good communication and assertiveness skills (see pages 13 and 22) to work things out. If you need help, you ask for it. You respect your teachers and classmates—and you expect respect in return.

DID YOU KNOW?

There are bullies in all walks of life: at home, at school, in the community, and even at work. Some bullies are young, and others are old.

Bullies want to control other people. They may be jealous of them. They may hate people who look and act differently from them. They may not have any self-respect, and they try to feel better about themselves by making someone else feel bad, or stronger by making someone else look weak. They may have been bullied themselves, and feel angry and frustrated. There are many possible reasons for bullying—but there is never an excuse for it. In the end, bullies hurt themselves as much as the victim; they will gain a life-long reputation for being a bully and miss out on good, lasting friendships.

You also pay attention in class, so you can learn as much as possible. You do your homework on time and prepare well for tests. You know how important it is to get the most out of every opportunity, because the person who will get the most benefit from all of this is you!

"Just as pain is not agreeable to you, it is so with others. Knowing this principle of equality, treat others with respect and compassion."

From the Samen Suttam, *the religious text of the Jainists*

Maintaining your self-respect in school will help you to reach your goals.

Respect in the Community

We all live in a community. It might be a town, a suburb, or a city, but we are all surrounded by other people. We are part of a society that has millions of other members.

A BIG MIX!

As we go through life, we come across thousands of other people. In our community, we see store clerks and bus drivers, and lots of the people who live near us. Sometimes we hardly notice them. Sometimes we greet them with a nod, a wave, or a quick "Hello." Sometimes we stop to talk with them.

Respect in the community goes a long way. Respectful relationships, no matter how brief they are, make life more enjoyable. Respect gives our contact with people a little more meaning.

Communities are full of people who are different from one another. Sometimes we can walk down a street and see people from different cultures wearing different clothes that reflect their own backgrounds and faiths. We may see people with disabilities: wheelchair users, partially sighted people with white sticks, or people with **Down's Syndrome**. We see people of all ages: babies in strollers, middle-aged businesspeople, and elderly people going about their lives. We see people who look rich and others who look poor.

Some people feel threatened or scared by people who look different from them. If they see someone in a wheelchair, they may try to avoid looking at him or her. Older people sometimes cross the road if they see a group of young people coming their way. But everyone in a community is special and has something good to offer. And everyone deserves respect.

Racism

Some people in society are **racist**. They look down on or feel scared by people who are a different color from them, come from a different country, or have a different faith. Children often pick up ideas like this from their families or friends. If they got to know the people they think they hate, they may find that they actually like them. Accepting people's differences is a key part of respect.

With so many people from different walks of life living alongside each other, respect is essential.

Try not to make assumptions about people you do not know. For example, some people think that homeless people are lazy or stupid because they do not have a job or a home, or that they are all **alcoholics** or drug users. However, many people are homeless through no fault of their own. Their families may have broken up, or they may have lost their jobs, and so they lose confidence and self-respect. This can make it hard for them to go forward in life. Be careful never to make judgments before you know the full story.

TIP

RESPECT IN OUR EVERYDAY LIVES

Without respect, society would collapse. If everyone acted as if they were the only important person on Earth, doing what they wanted and forgetting that they have responsibilities to other people, life would get very difficult. If people did not respect laws about speed limits, for example, people could get hurt or killed. Respect is not only important for relationships with our families and friends, in schools, and in the community—it is essential to keeping the world running safely and smoothly.

Showing respect in the community

It takes very little to show respect in our community. Speaking to people politely is a good start. In a store, it is polite and respectful to say "Please" and "Thank you" to the store clerk. Holding the door open for someone is a simple way to show respect, too. If you see people you recognize, you could try greeting them in a small way. Say "Hi!" or smile at them. Elderly people often enjoy talking to people when they are out. They may live alone and feel lonely at home.

Getting it Right

If you see a child who has fallen over in the street or fallen off a swing in the park, what do you do? Do you ignore her, because you are going somewhere or because you feel too embarrassed to ask if she needs help? Do you assume that she is OK and that you don't need to do anything?

It only takes a moment to help someone in need. If you stop to think about what they may need and how you can help them, it shows that you respect them, even if you don't know them. You could ask them quietly and politely if they need your help. They may be relieved and happy that you are willing to help. If they don't need you to do anything, you have lost nothing. They (and you) will feel better, just because you tried.

When we remember that everyone has feelings, needs, and problems—just like us—respect follows naturally. And a little bit of respect makes a big difference.

Taking the time to help others is respectful and gives everyone a good feeling.

Being thoughtful

It is respectful to consider other people's needs when we are out and about. On **public transportation**, try giving up your seat to people who look as if they need it more than you—an elderly or pregnant person, for example. Playing music loudly or using your cell phone can disturb other people in public places, such as a library. Shouting and fooling around with friends when walking down the street or in a park can make some people feel nervous.

YOUNG AND OLD

Sometimes young people feel annoyed that they are expected to respect older people, because they think that they are often not respected in return. They think that respect should be a two-way street! Some young people complain that adults always assume the worst of them and that elderly people are rude to them.

It is a sad fact that young people can sometimes be made to feel like second-class citizens in society. Often it seems that newspapers and televison programs focus exclusively on negative stories about young people's behavior—for instance their involvement in **vandalism**, **shoplifting**, alcohol, and drugs. This can cause older people to get the idea that all young people behave in the same way. It makes them fearful, and they lose all respect.

Earning respect

Of course, the majority of kids are not involved in crime, alcohol, or drugs. It is also true that the young deserve to be treated with as much respect as older people. Respect has nothing to do with age. However, respect does need to be earned. It is also important to show respect for others, even if respect is not given in return. If young people consistently show that they respect their communities, respect for young people will follow.

Getting it Right

Joe lives near the ocean. He likes to go to the beach on weekends—surfing and playing volleyball or football with his friends. At school one day, Joe's teacher told the class about a community volunteer project to clean up the beach. The previous week, one of Joe's friends had cut his foot badly on a broken glass bottle left lying in the sand. Joe and his friends decided to get involved. About 40 people, both adults and kids, got together on the day of the clean-up. For a whole afternoon they worked hard picking up litter. Joe enjoyed meeting the other volunteers and making new friends with similar interests. It was a great day—and the beach looked so much better by the end that Joe felt really proud to have made a real difference to a place he cares about.

Get involved!

Some communities have a variety of different groups and activities—for example, fundraising for something that the community desperately needs. Some communities have "clean-up" days when volunteers get together to clear litter from streets, parks, or beaches.

Joining in activities such as these is a way to show people that you care about the community you live in, and this will build mutual respect.

Community activities help to build respect between people of different age groups.

Respecting the Environment

Respect for our fellow humans makes the world a better place to live in. Everyone has an equal right to live on Earth and an equal right to be respected. But we all need to respect the planet we live on, too. Earth gives us all life—we could not live without it! Respect for our planet starts with respecting our environment.

THINK GLOBALLY, ACT LOCALLY!

Over six billion people live on Earth and, by 2050, experts think there will be over nine billion. The world's population is growing all the time, but the planet is not getting any bigger. We all depend on natural resources (for example oil, gas, and water) for the most basic activities in life, such as food, water, and shelter, and for work and leisure. The world's natural resources are limited, and they will not last forever. We each have a responsibility to find ways to use these resources carefully in order to make them last as long as possible. There are a lot of things that we can do to help, and small steps add up to make a big difference.

In Kenya, people have a saying: "We have not inherited this land from our ancestors; rather, we have borrowed it from our children." When we respect the environment, we respect Earth and all the people who will live here in the future.

We can respect the environment and the wider world with simple steps taken locally. There is a lot we can do at home and at school to save water and **energy** from gas, electricity, and oil.

Saving water

At home, we can take showers instead of baths and make sure we do not leave the faucet running when brushing our teeth or washing dishes.

DID YOU KNOW?

What do we mean by the word "environment"? It means the land that makes up the world's continents and islands; the water that makes up the oceans, lakes, rivers, and ice caps; and the air we all breathe. The environment also includes the billions of plants and animals on Earth. Humans have a responsibility to respect the environment, so that it stays healthy and balanced.

We should fix leaking faucets as quickly as possible. By keeping tap water in a jug in the refrigerator, there will always be cold water to drink, so we don't have to run a faucet for long.

Collecting rainwater for watering garden plants at home and at school is a useful way to save water. We could also plant drought-resistant plants that do not need much watering in our yards.

A rain barrel is simple to install and is a great way to collect rain from roofs and gutters to use on garden plants.

Saving energy

We can all help to save energy by switching lights off when they are not needed. Electrical products, such as televisions, use almost as much energy on standby as when they are on, so switching them off completely helps, too. And rather than turning the heating up when we feel cool, we can wear a sweater to stay warm.

Cars use a lot of gasoline, which is made from oil. Sometimes cars are needed because there is no alternative. However, many places have public transportation, such as buses and trains. Using public transportation whenever possible is good for the environment. If you are close enough to school and local stores, you can walk or cycle there. This saves gas and keeps you fit, too!

Buying local products is another good way to save energy. Local products do not have to be flown or driven to where you are, saving a lot of oil. Shopping for fruits and vegetables from local producers—or even growing your own—is a great way to help the environment.

Less is more

In today's world, people often buy and own a great deal: clothes, games, cell phones, electrical items, such as computers and MP3 players . . . the list goes on. We often change old items for new ones, even when the old ones are still perfectly OK.

Thrift stores and flea markets are a great source of interesting and good-quality clothes at very low prices!

Ads on television and in magazines make new items seem irresistible. People can feel that they are missing out if they do not own the latest product. However, if we think seriously about it, we do not really need a new cell phone if our old one still works. We do not really have to change our sneakers for the latest style. We are just persuaded by clever **advertisers** to think that we do.

Ideally, it would be great if people would stop buying things unnecessarily. Sometimes, though, it can be hard to resist the temptation or the pressure. If you do buy something new, it is a good idea to give your old item to someone else. Thrift stores, garage sales, and flea markets are good ways to recycle old belongings that are still in good condition. Someone can make good use of most of the things you no longer want. By recycling them, you respect other people and the environment.

Getting it
Right

When Naomi cleared out her room, she was amazed at how much stuff she had. She didn't want or need 10 pairs of shoes or 20 T-shirts! Naomi decided to hold a swap party with her friends so they could swap all their clothes. Everyone had fun and saved money at the same time.

Less waste, please!

Recycling is an easy way to respect the environment. Instead of using new plastic bags every time we shop, we can reuse old ones or use long-lasting bags made from materials other than plastic. Instead of buying bottled water, we can drink tap water. Instead of throwing away books, paper, aluminum foil, cans, glass, and plastic bottles, clothes, and old bedding, we can put them in recycling bins or give them to charity. Recycling is a great way to reduce waste and to protect the environment.

Every time you recycle something, you show that you respect Earth.

Improving our local environment

There is a domino effect to respecting the environment: our actions make our communities nicer places to live. Communities that have trees, grass, and flowers that are well maintained help people to relax and enjoy themselves. These areas attract insects, birds, and other animals, helping people remember they are part of nature.

People who live in places that are cared for often feel happier. Communities that are clear of litter, graffiti, and broken windows make people feel more valued—and even safer. When communities work to limit pollution, air and water are cleaner and people are healthier.

 **QUIZ**

DO YOU RESPECT THE ENVIRONMENT?

1) At school, you see that one of the faucets is leaking. You:
a) tell your teacher, so that he or she can arrange to have it fixed.
b) forget about it; you are sure that someone else will notice it and figure it out.

2) You are in the park and you see some people you know breaking the windows in the public restrooms. You:
a) tell a trusted adult, such as a parent, and ask him or her to report the incident to the police.
b) think it looks like fun and try it yourself.

3) You have just eaten an ice-cream cone and you want to get rid of the garbage. You:
a) look for a trash can and, if you can't see one, put the trash in your bag or pocket to throw away at home.
b) throw it on the ground; someone else will pick it up.

4) You decide that you are bored with the blue T-shirt you bought a month ago. You:
a) swap it with something else a friend has or donate it to a thrift store.
b) throw it in the garbage.

5) You have a cell phone that is a year old and your cell phone company allows you to change it for a new one. You:
a) Change your phone, but give your old one to charity.
b) get a new one as quickly as possible; you wouldn't be seen dead with an old-fashioned phone!

See quiz results on page 50.

Respecting Your Body

We have learned that when you respect yourself, you take care of yourself in different ways. You take care of your mind by taking part fully in school and taking the opportunities life brings you to learn and gain new skills. You care for yourself psychologically and emotionally by interacting with people and doing activities that make you feel good about yourself. And you care for your body, too: by having good **personal hygiene**, enough rest, a healthy diet, and plenty of exercise—and by avoiding unhealthy substances that can harm you.

A Healthy Approach

You only get one body to last you a lifetime, so it is important to take care of it and keep it as healthy as possible. Be careful about personal hygiene by washing, bathing, and brushing your teeth regularly. If you feel unwell, do what you need to get better. Go to the doctor, if necessary, and follow his or her advice. You should also have regular dental checkups to make sure that your teeth and gums stay healthy.

Rest and sleep

Rest is important for everyone, at any age. Time out is time to relax, and this gives you space to stop and think about things for a while. If you respect yourself, you try to make sure that you build in enough rest time in your day. You also make sure that you get enough sleep, which helps to keep you mentally and physically healthy and strong.

Exercise for life

Exercise is a key part of staying fit and healthy. When you have self-respect, you know that it is important for your body that you make time for exercise throughout your life. Exercise can beat disease, reduce stress, and improve sleep. It also sharpens your mind so that you will find it easier to concentrate. It is fun, too!

Try to put at least one hour aside each day to do some form of exercise.

You can get exercise in lots of different ways. At school, you can participate in team sports—such as soccer, hockey, volleyball, track, or tennis. Outside school hours you can walk, cycle, run, or swim to get the exercise your body needs. It is important to enjoy your chosen exercise. The more you like the exercise you do, the more you are likely to stick to it and reap the benefits it brings.

Healthy eating

Eating a healthy diet is another important way to respect our bodies. Messages about healthy eating are all around us. At the same time, everywhere we turn we are surrounded by unhealthy fast foods and drinks, such as chips, chocolate, candy, and soda.

It can be tempting to eat fast foods that taste good and give us a quick burst of energy. However, it is much more important to give our bodies the healthiest food we can. Food is like a fuel; our bodies need the right fuel in order to work in the right way. To stay healthy, we need to eat foods that give us plenty of **nutrients**. Eating three regular meals a day that contain a good variety of foods helps us to get all the nutrients we need and keeps our energy levels steady.

Being overweight

If you look around you, you will see that people's bodies come in all shapes and sizes. This is perfectly normal. However, some people are the wrong weight for their height.

A healthy, balanced diet with plenty of fruits and vegetables is important for a lifestyle of self-respect!

More and more young people today are becoming overweight or **obese**. Being overweight can lead to health problems, such as heart disease, diabetes, and cancer.

No one needs to be sad or embarrassed that they are overweight. However, if you are not at the right weight, you could think about making changes to your diet and exercise routine so that you can get healthier and fitter. This will show that you have lots of self-respect.

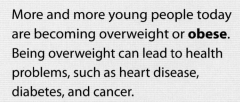

If you are overweight, you may want to exercise, but you may not know where to start. You may find it too tiring or difficult to play a team sport, such as basketball. Don't worry—exercise is for everyone! You just need to find the right kind of exercise for you. When you are unfit, it is a good idea to start with very gentle exercise. Walking just 20 minutes per day will make a real difference in your fitness. You can start off slowly and, as you get fitter, you can speed up. Walking is great because it takes you outdoors into the fresh air. And if you walk with a family member or a friend, you can talk as you walk! You will be able to support each other as you get fitter and healthier.

Being underweight

Some people think that it is cool to be skinny. After all, so many super-models and celebrities look like this. Sadly, many of the photos we see of famous people have been changed by computers to make them look thinner. We try to live up to an impossible image.

By trying to become thin, many people lose too much weight. They drastically cut down how much they eat and become underweight. Being underweight can cause serious health problems. Very thin people can pick up infections more easily, and their bones may become weak and break more easily.

Unhealthy substances

Tobacco, alcohol, and other drugs are all substances that can have a disastrous effect on health. All three are highly **addictive** and can destroy people's health, relationships, and their lives as a whole. In some cases, alcohol, tobacco, or drug abuse can lead to death from illnesses, such as heart disease and cancer, or **overdoses**.

Some drugs, such as tobacco and alcohol, are legal for adults. Others, such as cocaine and heroin, are illegal for everyone. But all drugs—legal or not—can be very unhealthy. The effects of drugs are even worse when young people use them. Because young people's bodies and brains are

DID YOU KNOW?

Eating disorders, especially anorexia and bulimia, are a growing problem for young people. Anorexia is when people severely restrict how much they eat because they are terrified about gaining weight. Bulimia is when people eat a lot of food and then vomit or use laxatives so that the food does not make them gain weight. Eating disorders are very serious problems, and left unmanaged, can lead to severe health problems—and even death. If you suspect you have (or a friend has) an eating disorder, you should seek professional help immediately.

still growing, they are more likely to suffer worse effects from unhealthy substances.

People often try drugs because they are curious, because they want to escape from problems or boredom, or because drugs seem exciting. Many young people come under pressure to try drugs from people they know. Self-respect helps people to resist such negative peer pressure.

One of the very best things we can do to respect ourselves is to steer clear of drugs. By doing this, we also show respect for the people we care about—because by ruining our own lives, we would ruin theirs, too.

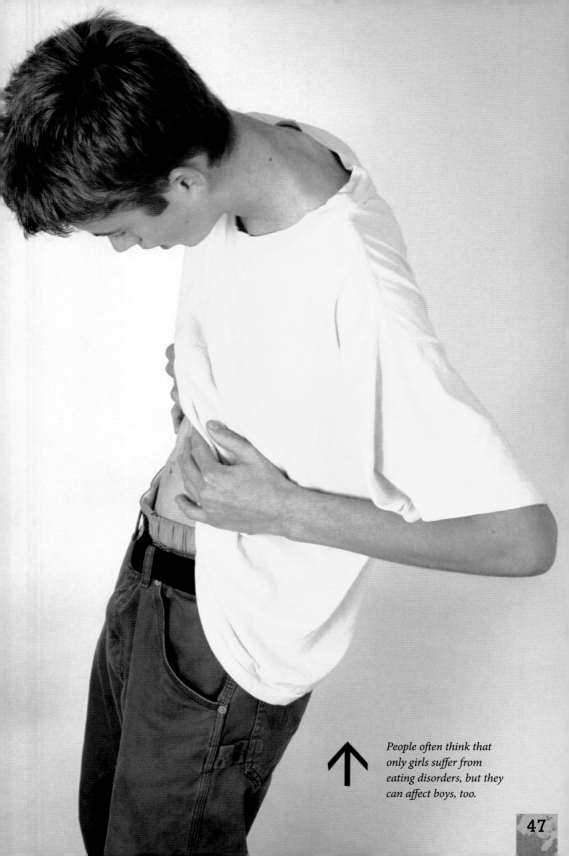

People often think that
only girls suffer from
eating disorders, but they
can affect boys, too.

Conclusion

Respect and self-respect are essential ingredients for a happy, healthy life. When we respect and accept ourselves for who we are ("warts and all!") we start to understand that everyone is important, with their own thoughts, feelings, needs, and wants. We appreciate that everyone is of equal value and deserves to be treated respectfully—no matter what they look like, what they do, or what they own.

POSITIVE THINKING

Self-respect helps us to see ourselves in a positive way, no matter what other people think of us. We know that we can change the things we need to change and that no one is ever perfect.

Respect for others improves our relationships with everyone we know and come across, from our families to our friends, our teachers, and our local communities.

Respect for the environment makes us feel part of something that is much bigger than ourselves. It gives us the satisfaction of knowing that we can contribute to making a positive difference to Earth and all the people that live here, now and in the future.

The lessons of respect

Allowing respect to become a fundamental part of our lives is very exciting. It leads the way to a host of good things that make our lives more fulfilled, more satisfying, and more contented.

We can learn assertiveness and good communication skills so that we can deal with problems with other people respectfully and in a way that shows we care about everyone involved. We can learn how to handle negative peer pressure, which will help us always to get the best out of—and give the best to—our friendships. Best of all, we realize that it is possible for us to take action to help the wider world.

The world is a better place when people respect one another and respect themselves, too.

Evan lives in a **multicultural** city and goes to a multicultural school. He is part of a big group of friends—boys and girls—who come from many different backgrounds, from Mexico, China, India, and Poland. It is a great mix, and everyone brings something different to the group. No one thinks that anyone is weird just because they look different or eat different foods. No one feels left out. Each person likes and respects the others exactly as they are.

Getting it
Right

IS RESPECT WORKING IN YOUR FAMILY?
For page 17

- **If you answered mainly a)s:**
Respect isn't part of your vocabulary! You do not seem to think much about how the things you do or say affect the people in your family. Think harder: if you respect your family members, you get more respect in return.

- **If you answered mainly b)s:**
Going along with what other people want and then getting angry about it afterward is not really respectful. Remember, true respect means thinking about what people want or need, and doing it happily—but only if it does not upset you in the process.

- **If you answered mainly c)s:**
Good job! You do know how to show respect for people in your family—and you clearly know about self-respect, too. You think about what other people need and, if you do not understand, you talk to them to work things out.

DO YOU RESPECT YOUR FRIENDS? AND DO THEY RESPECT YOU?
For page 23

- **If you answered mainly a)s:**
You definitely know how to respect your friends—and yourself! And you also know how to be assertive. These skills will set you up really well for good friendships, now and in the future.

- **If you answered mainly b)s:**
You need to remember that life isn't all about you! When you just think about yourself, you are not respecting other people. Try to think about what they need, too.

- **If you answered mainly c)s:**
You seem to go along with what others want, but not what you want. Pretending that you are OK with something when you are not is not a good foundation for a healthy friendship. Remember that respect should be a two-way street.

DO YOU RESPECT THE ENVIROMENT?
For page 41

- **If you answered mainly a)s:**
Good job—you really care! You respect the environment and your local community, and you do all you can to help. People like you really can make a difference in the world.

- **If you answered mainly b)s:**
Uh oh—it seems as if you have a bit of a "who cares?" attitude. Respecting the environment may take a bit of effort or may go against some of the things you want, but in the long run, helping the planet will be better for you and everyone else. Try taking some of the small steps you can find on pages 36—41.

20 THINGS TO REMEMBER

1 Be happy with who you are.

2 Remember that what you do is not the same as who you are. We can all change our not-so-good points; it is all part of growing up and developing as a person, and it goes on throughout life!

3 Take care of your mind—do whatever you can to learn a lot and enjoy all the opportunities life offers.

4 Don't let people put you down. Use assertiveness skills to help you work out problems with other people.

5 Never measure yourself against others. Everyone is different, and no one is better than anyone else.

6 If people criticize you, think about what they have said. Then decide if they are right or wrong, and decide what you need to do.

7 Care for your body: eat healthily, enjoy lots of fun exercise, and avoid unhealthy substances.

8 Remember that other people may be different from you, but they are just as valuable and they all have good points.

9 Be polite to everyone you know and meet. No matter who they are, they will appreciate it—and it will make you feel good, too!

10 Remember that rules are there for a reason! Respecting rules can keep you and other people safe and can make life run more smoothly.

11 Use good communication skills so that everyone in a conversation feels heard and respected.

12 Don't borrow people's things without asking. When you do borrow something, be careful with it and return it when agreed.

13 Teasing and putting people down hurts. Never get involved with bullying of any kind.

14 Help people who need help in the best way you can. It may be by listening to them, doing something practical for them, or doing something fun with them so they can forget their problems for a while.

15 Know that what you do has an impact on the wider world.

16 Pick up any litter you see on the school grounds or on the street and put it in a trash can.

17 Get involved with other people to care for your local community. Help to plant flowers or trees, or take part in a "clean-up" event.

18 Reduce, reuse, recycle! Help to protect the world's resources by not being wasteful.

19 Keep the heating down. Dress more warmly if you are feeling chilly.

20 Switch off lights and electrical equipment when they are not being used.

Further Information

BOOKS

Ballard, Carol. *Food for Feeling Healthy* (*Making Healthy Food Choices*). Chicago: Heinemann Library, 2007.

DiBattista, Rosemary Genova. *Female Body Image: A Hot Issue* (*Hot Issues*). Berkeley Heights, N.J.: Enslow, 2002.

Doeden, Matt. *Stay Fit!: How You Can Get in Shape* (*Health Zone*). Minneapolis: Lerner, 2008.

Giddens, Sandra. *Making Smart Choices about Cigarettes, Drugs, and Alcohol*. New York: Rosen, 2008.

Lynette, Rachel. *Drugs* (*The Real Deal*). Chicago: Heinemann Library, 2008.

Silverman, Buffy. *Recycling: Reducing Waste* (*Do It Yourself*). Chicago: Heinemann Library, 2009.

Todd, Ann Marie. *Get Green!* (*Life Skills*). Chicago: Heinemann Library, 2009.

WEBSITES

http://stopbullyingnow.hrsa.gov
This government website offers resources and information about bullying.

http://mypyramid.gov
This website offers advice on nutrition, exercise, and achieving a balanced diet through the "MyPyramid" food pyramid.

www.tobaccofreekids.org
The website for the Campaign for Tobacco-Free Kids offers facts and figures about the damage caused by smoking, as well as information about campaigns to raise awareness among kids.

www.foe.org
This website is for Friends of the Earth, a group that works to improve the state of the environment and people's health.

www.epa.gov/kids
This website of the U.S. Environmental Protection Agency is a good source for environmental information.

QUOTATIONS

Here are some quotes from some famous and not-so-famous people to help you to think about (and build) self-respect:

"No one can make you feel inferior without your permission."
[Eleanor Roosevelt, wife of U.S. President Franklin D. Roosevelt (1884–1962)]

"Never think that you're not good enough yourself. A man should never think that. People will take you very much at your own reckoning."
[Anthony Trollope, author (1815–1882)]

"I am sure it is one's duty as a teacher to try to show [students] that no opinions, no tastes, no emotions are worth much unless they are one's own."
[A. C. Benson, poet and author (1862–1925)]

"If you put a small value on yourself, rest assured that the world will not raise your price."
[Unknown]

"Low self-esteem is like driving through life with your hand-brake on."
[Maxwell Maltz, author and surgeon (1899–1975)]

"Nothing builds self-esteem and self-confidence like accomplishment."
[Thomas Carlyle, historian (1795–1881)]

"Let every man be respected as an individual and no man idolized."
[Albert Einstein, scientist (1879–1955)]

GLOSSARY

abuse treating someone badly. Abuse can be emotional, physical, or sexual.

addictive when a substance causes someone to not be able to stop using it

adoptive family family that has adopted a child. An adopted child is brought up legally by parents who did not give birth to the child.

advertiser person who makes advertisements to sell products to people

alcoholic someone who is addicted to alcohol

antisocial behavior actions that are harmful to society, such as vandalism

assertiveness confident behavior, shown when someone says what he or she thinks without being aggressive or passive

bully someone who hurts or scares someone with physical violence or words

community people who live in a particular place, such as a town or city

compromise when someone changes his or her opinion in order to reach an agreement with someone else

disability illness, condition, or injury that makes it hard for someone to do all the things that other people do

discipline take action to punish or correct someone who has done something wrong

divorced when a marriage has legally ended

Down's Syndrome condition that some people are born with, which causes them to have learning difficulties and health problems

energy power from something—for example, electricity or oil—that does work such as providing light and heat

faith particular religion, such as Christianity, Islam, or Buddhism

immigrant someone who has come to live in a particular country

laxative substance that helps people to empty their bowels

multicultural including people from different cultures

nutrient substance, such as a vitamin or mineral, that helps people to live and grow

obese very overweight

overdose when someone takes too much of a particular substance, especially a drug

peer pressure trying to influence someone of the same age to behave in the same way as yourself

personal hygiene keeping yourself clean and fresh through washing, bathing, wearing clean clothes, and so on

public transportation vehicles, such as buses and trains, that are used by the public and run on fixed routes at fixed times

racist someone who looks down on people from other countries and cultures

shoplifting illegally taking goods from a store without paying for them

sibling brother or sister

step-family family that includes one birth parent living with another adult and, possibly, the other adult's natural children

vandalism intentionally damaging someone else's property

Index